SELECTED POEMS OF

Carl Sandburg

SELECTED POEMS OF

Carl Sandburg

BARNES
&NOBLE
BOOKS
NEW YORK

Introduction copyright © 1994 by Barnes & Noble, Inc.
All rights reserved.

This edition published by Barnes & Noble, Inc.

1994 Barnes & Noble Books

ISBN 1-56619-264-1

Printed and bound in the United States of America

M   9   8   7   6   5   4   3 2

Contents

Introduction   xi

Chicago   1
Sketch   3
Masses   4
Lost   5
The Harbor   5
They Will Say   6
Halsted Street Car   7
Clark Street Bridge   8
Passers-by   9
A Teamster's Farewell   10
Fish Crier   10
Picnic Boat   11
Happiness   11
Graceland   12
The Right to Grief   13
Onion Days   15
Population Drifts   17
Cripple   18
Anna Imroth   18
Mamie   19
Cumulatives   20
Chamfort   21
Limited   22
The Has-Been   22
Dynamiter   23

 v

Ice Handler	24
Fellow Citizens	25
Style	27
To Beachey, 1912	28
In a Breath	29
Bronzes	30
Dunes	31
On the Way	32
Skyscraper	33
Fog	36
Pool	36
Choose	36
Whitelight	37
Flux	37
Troths	37
Iron	38
Fight	39
Buttons	40
Wars	41
The Road and the End	42
Graves	43
Aztec Mask	44
Who Am I?	45
Our Prayer of Thanks	46
At a Window	47
Under the Harvest Moon	48
The Great Hunt	49
Back Yard	50
Follies	51
Gone	52

Docks	53
Waiting	54
Dream Girl	55
I am the People, the Mob	56
Government	57
The Mist	58
Early Moon	59
Illinois Farmer	60
Hits and Runs	60
Sunset from Omaha Hotel Window	61
Bilbea	62
Portrait of a Motorcar	63
Sixteen Months	63
Prayers of Steel	64
Jabberers	65
Knucks	66
Testament	68
Crimson Rambler	69
Haunts	70
Have Me	70
Fire Dreams	71
Baby Face	72
The Year	73
Drumnotes	74
Cool Tombs	75
Shenandoah	76
New Feet	77
Old Osawatomie	77
Grass	78
Flanders	79

Old Timers   80
Remembered Women   81
A Million Young Workmen, 1915   82
The Four Brothers   83

Index of First Lines   89

Introduction

Carl Sandburg's idea of a complete poet was one who sang "of the quiet corner, of the green fields, and the earth serene in its changes" and "of streets and struggles, of dust and combat, of violence wanton or justified, of plain folk living close to a hard earth . . . ." Thus, he filled his poems with observations of people living in both the bare concrete confines of the city and the visionary landscapes of the countryside. Within either environs, Sandburg focused on both the failures and strengths of the common folk as they confronted the sometimes impenetrable circumstances surrounding their lives.

While other poets may write convincingly of Greek goddesses or of golden arrows, Sandburg's poetry is notable for its knuckled-down toughness and its unsentimental acceptance of his era's no-nonsense behavior. His poems diverge almost violently from the tradition of bards extending from the ancients to twentieth-century poets such as T. S. Eliot or Robert Frost. Sandburg greatly distrusted their use of rhyme or measured syllables to capture the complex struggles and hardships of the working men and women he saw about him. He complained that rhyme betrayed the poet's initial thoughts, as it was necessary to use only the words found fitting a rhyme instead of words that expressed a poet's first thought or feeling. A realist who wanted to capture a visceral response, he did not turn away from the social cruelties and misfortunes of his time to draw imaginary landscapes or pleasurable abodes. Sandburg dreamt, but his dream was of the people, the social Democratic dream as found in the Declaration of Independence, an ideal of "life, liberty, and the pursuit of happiness" for all.

He adopted his democratic and populist ideals from boyhood. Sandburg's parents migrated to the United States in the 1870s, leaving behind their ancestral ties to Sweden. They were pious, industrious people who worked hard to establish their family in the small town of Galesburg, Illinois. Carl Sandburg, born in 1878, was their eldest of three children. Even at the age of four, he was interested in the seemingly magical effect of words and books on the reader. When he learned to read, he frequently sought out books on the

American Revolutionaries and Civil War heroes. Reading the trials of the early patriots as a boy strengthened his sense of importance and self-worth. It encouraged him that he was fighting for the same aspirations as other young Americans had over a hundred years before him and that these aspirations were the same hopes and visions that Abraham Lincoln had sought to uphold.

During his school years, Sandburg took pleasure in reading as well as playing sports, but he would never finish high school. He often worked weekends to help support his family, but in the rough economic years following the Panic of 1893, tougher measures were required. His family's circumstances demanded that he quit school and work full-time. From the ages of fourteen to nineteen, he would have an innumerable array of occupations from an assistant to milkmen, barbers, potters, racetrack attendants, and a railroad section gang to working in a circus, a pop bottling shop, an ice-house, an auditorium, and the Kansas wheat fields during the harvest season.

His close affiliation with the people who worked with their hands brought him to understand and sympathize with many working-class people. These common folk—"The Hog Butcher, Tool Maker, Stacker of Wheat, Players with Railroads and Freight Handlers to the Nation"—he knew and admired. In his poems, he portrayed the Common Man as an individual who knows instinctively what's right and what's wrong. Hard-working and honest, they are aware of themselves as part of a larger social body, a greater humanity. Sandburg characterizes them as poets of experience who perceive the world with a rich, lusty vision, pulsating all about them with life. Their pursuit of happiness he summed up as an earthly revelry—in his poem "Happiness," they are "a crowd of Hungarians under the trees with their women and children and a keg of beer and an accordion."

To capture this elusive, ever-active throng of the masses, Sandburg adapted the multiple roles of the poet to his singular vision. In these selected poems, he has invoked the poet as pedestrian, nightwalker, searcher, eyewitness, traveler, working-class hero, day-dreamer, mourner, portrayer of urban and rural landscapes, and a mystic player of Masques chanting "I am the people . . . I am the audience . . . I am the mist . . . I am the grass."

Although he wrote about the people who will never leave their names to history, there is something lasting, something timeless about this body politic. In "Aztec Mask," this lastingness is desired, described, and found in an ancient

X

mask winning its precarious gamble against the passing hours. In "The Has-Been," a young man who repeatedly tries to deface the statue of a primitive god fails to erase its mystery contained within. With poems such as "Wars" or "On the Way," he drew correspondences between civilizations of the past and his contemporary America. As these poems show, Sandburg had a strong belief in the destiny and future of the people. He realized that this conviction could never be proven, but he never once doubted its power to move people towards acts of human compassion and change.

Sandburg was undoubtedly a populist, but he also recognized the importance of unique individuals, historically and artistically, who could realize some dream, some great cause "not yet dreamed out in the heads of men." As in the poem "Bronzes," a statue of General Ulysses S. Grant is described as shrinking behind the comings and goings of the people busy with their personal concerns. Yet at dusk and nightfall, when the masses prepare themselves for sleep, the sculpture of Grant is described as growing in stature, still calling out to those about him and daring them to ride "out into the hoofs and guns of the storm." It was his belief that Ulysses S. Grant was not only a shaper of the American Dream but also a product of the American Dream.

Written during the first decade of the century, the poems presented here—selected from Sandburg's "Chicago Poems," "Cornhuskers," and "Steam and Steel"—define a Chicago that has drastically changed. At times, Sandburg's work almost appears to be a document of his era. Yet, he also managed to capture in these urban poems the mysterious spirit of something existing beyond the passing day—those failed dreams and yearnings of city life—that return to America's troubled cities a sense of their awesome wonder.

—Robert Yagley
1994

xi

SELECTED POEMS OF

Carl Sandburg

Chicago

Hog Butcher for the World,
Tool Maker, Stacker of Wheat,
Player with Railroads and the Nation's Freight Handler;
Stormy, husky, brawling,
City of the Big Shoulders:

They tell me you are wicked and I believe them, for I have seen your painted
women under the gas lamps luring the farm boys.
And they tell me you are crooked and I answer: Yes, it is true I have seen the
gunman kill and go free to kill again.
And they tell me you are brutal and my reply is: On the faces of women and
children I have seen the marks of wanton hunger.
And having answered so I turn once more to those who sneer at this my city,
and I give them back the sneer and say to them:
Come and show me another city with lifted head singing so proud to be alive
and coarse and strong and cunning.
Flinging magnetic curses amid the toil of piling job on job, here is a tall bold
slugger set vivid against the little soft cities;
Fierce as a dog with tongue lapping for action, cunning as a savage pitted
against the wilderness,
        Bareheaded,
        Shoveling,
        Wrecking,
        Planning,
        Building, breaking, rebuilding,
Under the smoke, dust all over his mouth, laughing with white teeth,
Under the terrible burden of destiny laughing as a young man laughs,
Laughing even as an ignorant fighter laughs who has never lost a battle,

Bragging and laughing that under his wrist is the pulse, and under his ribs the
heart of the people,
Laughing!
Laughing the stormy, husky, brawling laughter of Youth, half-naked, sweating,
proud to be Hog Butcher, Tool Maker, Stacker of Wheat, Player with
Railroads and Freight Handler to the Nation.

Sketch

The shadows of the ships
Rock on the crest
In the low blue lustre
Of the tardy and the soft inrolling tide.

A long brown bar at the dip of the sky
Puts an arm of sand in the span of salt.

The lucid and endless wrinkles
Draw in, lapse and withdraw.
Wavelets crumble and white spent bubbles
Wash on the floor of the beach.

    Rocking on the crest
    In the low blue lustre
    Are the shadows of the ships.

Masses

Among the mountains I wandered and saw blue haze and red crag and was
  amazed;
On the beach where the long push under the endless tide maneuvers, I stood
  silent;
Under the stars on the prairie watching the Dipper slant over the horizon's
  grass, I was full of thoughts.
Great men, pageants of war and labor, soldiers and workers, mothers lifting
  their children—these all I touched, and felt the solemn thrill of them.
And then one day I got a true look at the Poor, millions of the Poor, patient
  and toiling; more patient than crags, tides, and stars; innumerable,
  patient as the darkness of night—and all broken, humble ruins of nations.

Lost

Desolate and lone
All night long on the lake
Where fog trails and mist creeps,
The whistle of a boat
Calls and cries unendingly,
Like some lost child
In tears and trouble
Hunting the harbor's breast
And the harbor's eyes.

The Harbor

Passing through huddled and ugly walls
By doorways where women
Looked from their hunger-deep eyes,
Haunted with shadows of hunger-hands,
Out from the huddled and ugly walls,
I came sudden, at the city's edge,
On a blue burst of lake,
Long lake waves breaking under the sun
On a spray-flung curve of shore;
And a fluttering storm of gulls,
Masses of great gray wings
And flying white bellies
Veering and wheeling free in the open.

They Will Say

Of my city the worst that men will ever say is this:
You took little children away from the sun and the dew,
And the glimmers that played in the grass under the great sky,
And the reckless rain; you put them between walls
To work, broken and smothered, for bread and wages,
To eat dust in their throats and die empty-hearted
For a little handful of pay on a few Saturday nights.

Halsted Street Car

Come you, cartoonists,
Hang on a strap with me here
At seven o'clock in the morning
On a Halsted street car.

Take your pencils
And draw these faces.

Try with your pencils for these crooked faces,
That pig-sticker in one corner—his mouth—
That overall factory girl—her loose cheeks.

Find for your pencils
A way to mark your memory
Of tired empty faces.

After their night's sleep,
In the moist dawn
And cool daybreak,
    Faces
Tired of wishes,
Empty of dreams.

Clark Street Bridge

Dust of the feet
And dust of the wheels,
Wagons and people going,
All day feet and wheels.

Now . . .
. . . Only stars and mist
A lonely policeman,
Two cabaret dancers,
Stars and mist again,
No more feet or wheels,
No more dust and wagons.

    Voices of dollars
    And drops of blood
    . . . . . .
    Voices of broken hearts,
    . . . Voices singing, singing,
    . . . Silver voices, singing,
    Softer than the stars,
    Softer than the mist.

Passers-by

Passers-by,
Out of your many faces
Flash memories to me
Now at the day end
Away from the sidewalks
Where your shoe soles traveled
And your voices rose and blent
To form the city's afternoon roar
Hindering an old silence.

Passers-by,
I remember lean ones among you,
Throats in the clutch of a hope,
Lips written over with strivings,
Mouths that kiss only for love,
Records of great wishes slept with,
 Held long
And prayed and toiled for:

 Yes,
Written on
Your mouths
And your throats
I read them
When you passed by.

A Teamster's Farewell

SOBS EN ROUTE TO A PENITENTIARY

Good-by now to the streets and the clash of wheels and locking hubs,
The sun coming on the brass buckles and harness knobs,
The muscles of the horses sliding under their heavy haunches,
Good-by now to the traffic policeman and his whistle,
The smash of the iron hoof on the stones,
All the crazy wonderful slamming roar of the street—
O God, there's noises I'm going to be hungry for.

Fish Crier

I know a Jew fish crier down on Maxwell Street with a voice like a north wind
blowing over corn stubble in January.
He dangles herring before prospective customers evincing a joy identical with
that of Pavlowa dancing.
His face is that of a man terribly glad to be selling fish, terribly glad that God
made fish, and customers to whom he may call his wares from a pushcart.

Picnic Boat

Sunday night and the park policemen tell each other it is dark as a stack of
   black cats on Lake Michigan.
A big picnic boat comes home to Chicago from the peach farms of Saugatuck.
Hundreds of electric bulbs break the night's darkness, a flock of red and yellow
   birds with wings at a standstill.
Running along the deck-railings are festoons and leaping in curves are loops
   of light from prow and stern to the tall smokestacks.
Over the hoarse crunch of waves at my pier comes a hoarse answer in the
   rhythmic oompa of the brasses playing a Polish folk-song for the
   home-comers.

Happiness

I asked professors who teach the meaning of life to tell me what is happiness.
And I went to famous executives who boss the work of thousands of men.
They all shook their heads and gave me a smile as though I was trying to fool
   with them.
And then one Sunday afternoon I wandered out along the Desplaines river
And I saw a crowd of Hungarians under the trees with their women and
   children and a keg of beer and an accordion.

Graceland

Tomb of a millionaire,
A multi-millionaire, ladies and gentlemen,
Place of the dead where they spend every year
The usury of twenty-five thousand dollars
    For upkeep and flowers
To keep fresh the memory of the dead.
The merchant prince gone to dust
Commanded in his written will
Over the signed name of his last testament
Twenty-five thousand dollars be set aside
For roses, lilacs, hydrangeas, tulips,
For perfume and color, sweetness of remembrance
Around his last long home.

(A hundred cash girls want nickels to go to the movies tonight.
In the back stalls of a hundred saloons, women are at tables
Drinking with men or waiting for men jingling loose silver dollars in their
    pockets.
In a hundred furnished rooms is a girl who sells silk or dress goods or leather
    stuff for six dollars a week wages
And when she pulls on her stockings in the morning she is reckless about God
    and the newspapers and the police, the talk of her home town or the name
    people call her.)

The Right to Grief

TO CERTAIN POETS ABOUT TO DIE

Take your fill of intimate remorse, perfumed sorrow,
Over the dead child of a millionaire,
And the pity of Death refusing any check on the bank
Which the millionaire might order his secretary to scratch off
And get cashed.

  Very well,
You for your grief and I for mine.
Let me have a sorrow my own if I want to.

I shall cry over the dead child of a stockyards hunky.
His job is sweeping blood off the floor.
He gets a dollar seventy cents a day when he works
And it's many tubs of blood he shoves out with a broom day by day.

Now his three year old daughter
Is in a white coffin that cost him a week's wages.
Every Saturday night he will pay the undertaker fifty cents till the debt is
    wiped out.

The hunky and his wife and the kids
Cry over the pinched face almost at peace in the white box.
They remember it was scrawny and ran up high doctor bills.
They are glad it is gone for the rest of the family now will have more to eat
    and wear.

Yet before the majesty of Death they cry around the coffin
And wipe their eyes with red bandanas and sob when the priest says, "God
    have mercy on us all."

13

I have a right to feel my throat choke about this.

You take your grief and I mine—see?

Tomorrow there is no funeral and the hunky goes back to his job sweeping blood off the floor at a dollar seventy cents a day.

All he does all day long is keep on shoving hog blood ahead of him with a broom.

14

Onion Days

Mrs. Gabrielle Giovannitti comes along Peoria Street every morning at nine
o'clock
With kindling wood piled on top of her head, her eyes looking straight ahead
to find the way for her old feet.
Her daughter-in-law, Mrs. Pietro Giovannitti, whose husband was killed in a
tunnel explosion through the negligence of a fellow-servant,
Works ten hours a day, sometimes twelve, picking onions for Jasper on the
Bowmanville road.
She takes a street car at half-past five in the morning, Mrs. Pietro Giovannitti
does,
And gets back from Jasper's with cash for her day's work, between nine and
ten o'clock at night.
Last week she got eight cents a box, Mrs. Pietro Giovannitti, picking onions
for Jasper,
But this week Jasper dropped the pay to six cents a box because so many
women and girls were answering the ads in the *Daily News*.
Jasper belongs to an Episcopal church in Ravenswood and on certain Sundays
He enjoys chanting the Nicene creed with his daughters on each side of him
joining their voices with his.
If the preacher repeats old sermons of a Sunday, Jasper's mind wanders to his
700-acre farm and how he can make it produce more efficiently
And sometimes he speculates on whether he could word an ad in the *Daily
News* so it would bring more women and girls out to his farm and reduce
operating costs.
Mrs. Pietro Giovannitti is far from desperate about life; her joy is in a child
she knows will arrive to her in three months.
And now while these are the pictures for today there are other pictures of the
Giovannitti people I could give you for tomorrow,

And how some of them go to the county agent on winter mornings with their baskets for beans and cornmeal and molasses.

I listen to fellows saying here's good stuff for a novel or it might be worked up into a good play.

I say there's no dramatist living can put old Mrs. Gabrielle Giovannitti into a play with that kindling wood piled on top of her head coming along Peoria Street nine o'clock in the morning.

Population Drifts

New-mown hay smell and wind of the plain made her a woman whose ribs had the power of the hills in them and her hands were tough for work and there was passion for life in her womb.

She and her man crossed the ocean and the years that marked their faces saw them haggling with landlords and grocers while six children played on the stones and prowled in the garbage cans.

One child coughed its lungs away, two more have adenoids and can neither talk nor run like their mother, one is in jail, two have jobs in a box factory

And as they fold the pasteboard, they wonder what the wishing is and the wistful glory in them that flutters faintly when the glimmer of spring comes on the air or the green of summer turns brown:

They do not know it is the new-mown hay smell calling and the wind of the plain praying for them to come back and take hold of life again with tough hands and with passion.

Cripple

Once when I saw a cripple
Gasping slowly his last days with the white plague,
Looking from hollow eyes, calling for air,
Desperately gesturing with wasted hands
In the dark and dust of a house down in a slum,
I said to myself
I would rather have been a tall sunflower
Living in a country garden
Lifting a golden-brown face to the summer,
Rain-washed and dew-misted,
Mixed with the poppies and ranking hollyhocks,
And wonderingly watching night after night
The clear silent processionals of stars.

Anna Imroth

Cross the hands over the breast here—so.
Straighten the legs a little more—so.
And call for the wagon to come and take her home.
Her mother will cry some and so will her sisters
and brothers.
But all of the others got down and they are safe
    and this is the only one of the factory girls
    who wasn't lucky in making the jump
    when the fire broke.
It is the hand of God and the lack of fire escapes.

18

Mamie

Mamie beat her head against the bars of a little Indiana town and dreamed of
romance and big things off somewhere the way the railroad trains all ran.

She could see the smoke of the engines get lost down where the streaks of steel
flashed in the sun and when the newspapers came in on the morning mail
she knew there was a big Chicago far off, where all the trains ran.

She got tired of the barber shop boys and the post office chatter and the
church gossip and the old pieces the band played on the Fourth of July
and Decoration Day

And sobbed at her fate and beat her head against the bars and was going to
kill herself

When the thought came to her that if she was going to die she might as well
die struggling for a clutch of romance among the streets of Chicago.

She has a job now at six dollars a week in the basement of the Boston Store

And even now she beats her head against the bars in the same old way and
wonders if there is a bigger place the railroads run to from Chicago
where maybe there is
        romance
        and big things
        and real dreams
        that never go smash.

Cumulatives

Storms have beaten on this point of land
And ships gone to wreck here
      and the passers-by remember it
      with talk on the deck at night
      as they near it.

Fists have beaten on the face of this old prize-fighter
And his battles have held the sporting pages
      and on the street they indicate him with their
      right forefinger as one who once wore
      a championship belt.

A hundred stories have been published and a thousand rumored
About why this tall dark man has divorced two beautiful young women
And married a third who resembles the first two
      and they shake their heads and say, "There he goes,"
      when he passes by in sunny weather or in rain
      along the city streets.

Chamfort

There's Chamfort. He's a sample.
Locked himself in his library with a gun,
Shot off his nose and shot out his right eye.
And this Chamfort knew how to write
And thousands read his books on how to live,
But he himself didn't know
How to die by force of his own hand—see?
They found him a red pool on the carpet
Cool as an April forenoon,
Talking and talking gay maxims and grim epigrams.
Well, he wore bandages over his nose and right eye,
Drank coffee and chatted many years
With men and women who loved him
Because he laughed and daily dared Death:
"Come and take me."

Limited

I am riding on a limited express, one of the crack trains of the nation.
Hurtling across the prairie into blue haze and dark air go fifteen all-steel
coaches holding a thousand people.
(All the coaches shall be scrap and rust and all the men and women
laughing in the diners and sleepers shall pass to ashes.)
I ask a man in the smoker where he is going and he answers: "Omaha."

The Has-Been

A stone face higher than six horses stood five thousand years gazing at the
world seeming to clutch a secret.
A boy passes and throws a niggerhead that chips off the end of the nose from
the stone face; he lets fly a mud ball that spatters the right eye and cheek
of the old looker-on.
The boy laughs and goes whistling "ee-ee-ee ee-ee-ee." The stone face
stands silent, seeming to clutch a secret.

Dynamiter

I sat with a dynamiter at supper in a German saloon eating steak and onions.

And he laughed and told stories of his wife and children and the cause of labor
and the working class.

It was laughter of an unshakable man knowing life to be a rich and red-
blooded thing.

Yes, his laugh rang like the call of gray birds filled with a glory of joy ramming
their winged flight through a rain storm.

His name was in many newspapers as an enemy of the nation and few keepers
of churches or schools would open their doors to him.

Over the steak and onions not a word was said of his deep days and nights as
a dynamiter.

Only I always remember him as a lover of life, a lover of children, a lover of
all free, reckless laughter everywhere—lover of red hearts and red blood
the world over.

Ice Handler

I know an ice handler who wears a flannel shirt with pearl buttons the size of
a dollar,
And he lugs a hundred-pound hunk into a saloon icebox, helps himself to cold
ham and rye bread,
Tells the bartender it's hotter than yesterday and will be hotter yet tomorrow,
by Jesus,
And is on his way with his head in the air and a hard pair of fists.
He spends a dollar or so every Saturday night on a two hundred pound woman
who washes dishes in the Hotel Morrison.
He remembers when the union was organized he broke the noses of two scabs
and loosened the nuts so the wheels came off six different wagons one
morning, and he came around and watched the ice melt in the street.
All he was sorry for was one of the scabs bit him on the knuckles of the right
hand so they bled when he came around to the saloon to tell the boys
about it.

Fellow Citizens

I drank musty ale at the Illinois Athletic Club with the millionaire manufacturer of Green River butter one night
And his face had the shining light of an old-time Quaker, he spoke of a
beautiful daughter, and I knew he had a peace and a happiness up his
sleeve somewhere.
Then I heard Jim Kirch make a speech to the Advertising Association on the
trade resources of South America.
And the way he lighted a three-for-a-nickel stogie and cocked it at an angle
regardless of the manners of our best people,
I knew he had a clutch on a real happiness even though some of the reporters
on his newspaper say he is the living double of Jack London's Sea Wolf.
In the mayor's office the mayor himself told me he was happy though it is a
hard job to satisfy all the office-seekers and eat all the dinners he is asked
to eat.
Down in Gilpin Place, near Hull House, was a man with his jaw wrapped for
a bad toothache,
And he had it all over the butter millionaire, Jim Kirch and the mayor when
it came to happiness.
He is a maker of accordions and guitars and not only makes them from start
to finish, but plays them after he makes them.
And he had a guitar of mahogany with a walnut bottom he offered for seven
dollars and a half if I wanted it,
And another just like it, only smaller, for six dollars, though he never
mentioned the price till I asked him,
And he stated the price in a sorry way, as though the music and the make of
an instrument count for a million times more than the price in money.

I thought he had a real soul and knew a lot about God.

There was light in his eyes of one who has conquered sorrow in so far as sorrow is conquerable or worth conquering.

Anyway he is the only Chicago citizen I was jealous of that day.

He played a dance they play in some parts of Italy when the harvest of grapes is over and the wine presses are ready for work.

Style

Style—go ahead talking about style.
You can tell where a man gets his style just
    as you can tell where Pavlowa got her legs
    or Ty Cobb his batting eye.

    Go on talking.
Only don't take my style away.
      It's my face.
      Maybe no good
          but anyway, my face.
I talk with it, I sing with it, I see, taste and feel with it, I know why I want to
    keep it.

Kill my style
          and you break Pavlowa's legs,
          and you blind Ty Cobb's batting eye.

To Beachey, 1912

Riding against the east,
A veering, steady shadow
Purrs the motor-call
Of the man-bird
Ready with the death-laughter
In his throat
And in his heart always
The love of the big blue beyond.

Only a man,
A far fleck of shadow on the east
Sitting at ease
With his hands on a wheel
And around him the large gray wings.
Hold him, great soft wings,
Keep and deal kindly, O wings,
With the cool, calm shadow at the wheel.

In a Breath

TO THE WILLIAMSON BROTHERS

High noon. White sun flashes on the Michigan Avenue asphalt. Drum of hoofs and whirr of motors. Women trapesing along in flimsy clothes catching play of sun-fire to their skin and eyes.

Inside the playhouse are movies from under the sea. From the heat of pavements and the dust of sidewalks, passers-by go in a breath to be witnesses of large cool sponges, large cool fishes, large cool valleys and ridges of coral spread silent in the soak of the ocean floor thousands of years.

A naked swimmer dives. A knife in his right hand shoots a streak at the throat of a shark. The tail of the shark lashes. One swing would kill the swimmer. . . . Soon the knife goes into the soft underneck of the veering fish. . . . Its mouthful of teeth, each tooth a dagger itself, set row on row, glistens when the shuddering, yawning cadaver is hauled up by the brothers of the swimmer.

Outside in the street is the murmur and singing of life in the sun—horses, motors, women trapesing along in flimsy clothes, play of sun-fire in their blood.

Bronzes

I

The bronze General Grant riding a bronze horse in Lincoln Park
Shrivels in the sun by day when the motor cars whirr by in long processions
    going somewhere to keep appointments for dinner and matineés and
    buying and selling
Though in the dusk and nightfall when high waves are piling
On the slabs of the promenade along the lake shore near by
I have seen the general dare the combers come closer
And make to ride his bronze horse out into the hoofs and guns of the storm.

II

I cross Lincoln Park on a winter night when the snow is falling.
Lincoln in bronze stands among the white lines of snow, his bronze forehead
    meeting soft echoes of the newsies crying forty thousand men are dead
    along the Yser, his bronze ears listening to the mumbled roar of the city
    at his bronze feet.
A lithe Indian on a bronze pony, Shakespeare seated with long legs in bronze,
    Garibaldi in a bronze cape, they hold places in the cold, lonely snow
    tonight on their pedestals and so they will hold them past midnight and
    into the dawn.

Dunes

What do we see here in the sand dunes of the white moon alone with our
thoughts, Bill,
Alone with our dreams, Bill, soft as the women tying scarves around their
heads dancing,
Alone with a picture and a picture coming one after the other of all the dead,
The dead more than all these grains of sand one by one piled here in the
moon,
Piled against the sky-line taking shapes like the hand of the wind wanted,
What do we see here, Bill, outside of what the wise men beat their heads on,
Outside of what the poets cry for and the soldiers drive on headlong and leave
their skulls in the sun for—what, Bill?

On the Way

Little one, you have been buzzing in the books,
Flittering in the newspapers and drinking beer with lawyers
And amid the educated men of the clubs you have been getting an earful of
speech from trained tongues.
Take an earful from me once, go with me on a hike
Along sand stretches on the great inland sea here
And while the eastern breeze blows on us and the restless surge
Of the lake waves on the breakwater breaks with an ever fresh monotone,
Let us ask ourselves: What is truth? what do you or I know?
How much do the wisest of the world's men know about where the massed
human procession is going?

You have heard the mob laughed at?
I ask you: Is not the mob rough as the mountains are rough?
And all things human rise from the mob and relapse and rise again as rain to
the sea?

Skyscraper

By day the skyscraper looms in the smoke and sun and has a soul.

Prairie and valley, streets of the city, pour people into it and they mingle among its twenty floors and are poured out again back to the streets, prairies and valleys.

It is the men and women, boys and girls so poured in and out all day that give the building a soul of dreams and thoughts and memories.

(Dumped in the sea or fixed in a desert, who would care for the building or speak its name or ask a policeman the way to it?)

Elevators slide on their cables and tubes catch letters and parcels and iron pipes carry gas and water in and sewage out.

Wires climb with secrets, carry light and carry words, and tell terrors and profits and loves—curses of men grappling plans of business and questions of women in plots of love.

Hour by hour the caissons reach down to the rock of the earth and hold the building to a turning planet.

Hour by hour the girders play as ribs and reach out and hold together the stone walls and floors.

Hour by hour the hand of the mason and the stuff of the mortar clinch the pieces and parts to the shape an architect voted.

Hour by hour the sun and the rain, the air and the rust, and the press of time running into centuries, play on the building inside and out and use it.

Men who sunk the pilings and mixed the mortar are laid in graves where the wind whistles a wild song without words

And so are men who strung the wires and fixed the pipes and tubes and those who saw it rise floor by floor.

Souls of them all are here, even the hod carrier begging at back doors hundreds of miles away and the bricklayer who went to state's prison for shooting another man while drunk.

(One man fell from a girder and broke his neck at the end of a straight plunge—he is here—his soul has gone into the stones of the building.)

On the office doors from tier to tier—hundreds of names and each name standing for a face written across with a dead child, a passionate lover, a driving ambition for a million dollar business or a lobster's ease of life.

Behind the signs on the doors they work and the walls tell nothing from room to room.

Ten-dollar-a-week stenographers take letters from corporation officers, lawyers, efficiency engineers, and tons of letters go bundled from the building to all ends of the earth.

Smiles and tears of each office girl go into the soul of the building just the same as the master-men who rule the building.

Hands of clocks turn to noon hours and each floor empties its men and women who go away and eat and come back to work.

Toward the end of the afternoon all work slackens and all jobs go slower as the people feel day closing on them.

One by one the floors are emptied. . . . The uniformed elevator men are gone. Pails clang. . . . Scrubbers work, talking in foreign tongues. Broom and water and mop clean from the floors human dust and spit, and machine grime of the day.

Spelled in electric fire on the roof are words telling miles of houses and people where to buy a thing for money. The sign speaks till midnight.

Darkness on the hallways. Voices echo. Silence holds. . . . Watchmen walk slow from floor to floor and try the doors. Revolvers bulge from their hip pockets. . . . Steel safes stand in corners. Money is stacked in them.

A young watchman leans at a window and sees the lights of barges butting
their way across a harbor, nets of red and white lanterns in a railroad yard,
and a span of glooms splashed with lines of white and blurs of crosses and
clusters over the sleeping city.
By night the skyscraper looms in the smoke and the stars and has a soul.

Fog

The fog comes
on little cat feet.

It sits looking
over harbor and city
on silent haunches
and then moves on.

Pool

Out of the fire
Came a man sunken
To less than cinders,
A tea-cup of ashes or so.
And I,
The gold in the house,
Writhed into a stiff pool.

Choose

The single clenched fist lifted and ready,
Or the open asking hand held out and waiting.
Choose:
For we meet by one or the other.

Whitelight

Your whitelight flashes the frost tonight
Moon of the purple and silent west.
Remember me one of your lovers of dreams.

Flux

Sand of the sea runs red
Where the sunset reaches and quivers.
Sand of the sea runs yellow
Where the moon slants and wavers.

Troths

Yellow dust on a bumble
    bee's wing,
Grey lights in a woman's
    asking eyes,
Red ruins in the changing
    sunset embers:
I take you and pile high
    the memories.
Death will break her claws
    on some I keep.

Iron

Guns,
Long, steel guns,
Pointed from the war ships
In the name of the war god.
Straight, shining, polished guns,
Clambered over with jackies in white blouses,
Glory of tan faces, tousled hair, white teeth,
Laughing lithe jackies in white blouses,
Sitting on the guns singing war songs, war chanties.

Shovels,
Broad, iron shovels,
Scooping out oblong vaults,
Loosening turf and leveling sod.

I ask you
To witness—
The shovel is brother to the gun.

Fight

Red drips from my chin where I have been eating.
Not all the blood, nowhere near all, is wiped off my mouth.

Clots of red mess my hair
And the tiger, the buffalo, know how.

I was a killer.
        Yes, I am a killer.

I come from killing.
        I go to more.
I drive red joy ahead of me from killing.
Red gluts and red hungers run in the smears and juices of my inside bones:
The child cries for a suck mother and I cry for war.

Buttons

I have been watching the war map slammed up for advertising in front of the
newspaper office.
Buttons—red and yellow buttons—blue and black buttons—are shoved back
and forth across the map.

A laughing young man, sunny with freckles,
Climbs a ladder, yells a joke to somebody in the crowd,
And then fixes a yellow button one inch west
And follows the yellow button with a black button one inch west.

(Ten thousand men and boys twist on their bodies in a red soak along a river
edge,
Gasping of wounds, calling for water, some rattling death in their throats.)
Who would guess what it cost to move two buttons one inch on the war map
here in front of the newspaper office where the freckle-faced young man
is laughing to us?

Wars

In the old wars drum of hoofs and the beat of shod feet.
In the new wars hum of motors and the tread of rubber tires.
In the wars to come silent wheels and whirr of rods not yet dreamed out in the
heads of men.

In the old wars clutches of short swords and jabs into faces with spears.
In the new wars long-range guns and smashed walls, guns running a spit of
metal and men falling in tens and twenties.
In the wars to come new silent deaths, new silent hurlers not yet dreamed out
in the heads of men.

In the old wars kings quarreling and thousands of men following.
In the new wars kings quarreling and millions of men following.
In the wars to come kings kicked under the dust and millions of men following
great causes not yet dreamed out in the heads of men.

The Road and the End

I shall foot it
Down the roadway in the dusk,
Where shapes of hunger wander
And the fugitives of pain go by.
I shall foot it
In the silence of the morning,
See the night slur into dawn,
Hear the slow great winds arise
Where tall trees flank the way
And shoulder toward the sky.

The broken boulders by the road
Shall not commemorate my ruin.
Regret shall be the gravel under foot.
I shall watch for
Slim birds swift of wing
That go where wind and ranks of thunder
Drive the wild processionals of rain.

The dust of the traveled road
Shall touch my hands and face.

Graves

I dreamed one man stood against a thousand,
One man damned as a wrongheaded fool.
One year and another he walked the streets,
And a thousand shrugs and hoots
Met him in the shoulders and mouths he passed.

He died alone
And only the undertaker came to his funeral.

Flowers grow over his grave anod in the wind,
And over the graves of the thousand, too,
The flowers grow anod in the wind.

Flowers and the wind,
Flowers anod over the graves of the dead,
Petals of red, leaves of yellow, streaks of white,
Masses of purple sagging . . .
I love you and your great way of forgetting.

Aztec Mask

I wanted a man's face looking into the jaws and throat of life
With something proud on his face, so proud no smash of the jaws,
No gulp of the throat leaves the face in the end
With anything else than the old proud look:
      Even to the finish, dumped in the dust,
      Lost among the used-up cinders,
      This face, men would say, is a flash,
      Is laid on bones taken from the ribs of the earth,
      Ready for the hammers of changing, changing years,
      Ready for the sleeping, sleeping years of silence.
      Ready for the dust and fire and wind.
I wanted this face and I saw it today in an Aztec mask.
A cry out of storm and dark, a red yell and a purple prayer,
A beaten shape of ashes
        waiting the sunrise or night,
        something or nothing,
        proud-mouthed,
        proud-eyed gambler.

Who Am I?

My head knocks against the stars.
My feet are on the hilltops.
My finger-tips are in the valleys and shores of universal life.
Down in the sounding foam of primal things I reach my hands and play
    with pebbles of destiny.
I have been to hell and back many times.
I know all about heaven, for I have talked with God.
I dabble in the blood and guts of the terrible.
I know the passionate seizure of beauty
And the marvelous rebellion of man at all signs reading "Keep Off."

My name is Truth and I am the most elusive captive in the universe.

Our Prayer of Thanks

For the gladness here where the sun is shining at evening on the weeds at the
    river,
    Our prayer of thanks.

For the laughter of children who tumble barefooted and bareheaded in the
    summer grass,
    Our prayer of thanks.

For the sunset and the stars, the women and the white arms that hold us,
    Our prayer of thanks.

God,
If you are deaf and blind, if this is all lost to you,
God, if the dead in their coffins amid the silver handles on the edge of town,
    or the reckless dead of war days thrown unknown in pits, if these dead
    are forever deaf and blind and lost,
    Our prayer of thanks.

God,
The game is all your way, the secrets and the signals and the system; and so
    for the break of the game and the first play and the last.
    Our prayer of thanks.

◢ 46

At a Window

Give me hunger,
O you gods that sit and give
The world its orders.
Give me hunger, pain and want,
Shut me out with shame and failure
From your doors of gold and fame,
Give me your shabbiest, weariest hunger!

But leave me a little love,
A voice to speak to me in the day end,
A hand to touch me in the dark room
Breaking the long loneliness.
In the dusk of day-shapes
Blurring the sunset,
One little wandering, western star
Thrust out from the changing shores of shadow.
Let me go to the window,
Watch there the day-shapes of dusk
And wait and know the coming
Of a little love.

Under the Harvest Moon

Under the harvest moon,
When the soft silver
Drips shimmering
Over the garden nights,
Death, the gray mocker,
Comes and whispers to you
As a beautiful friend
Who remembers.

Under the summer roses
When the flagrant crimson
Lurks in the dusk
Of the wild red leaves,
Love, with little hands,
Comes and touches you
With a thousand memories,
And asks you
Beautiful, unanswerable questions.

The Great Hunt

I cannot tell you now;
    When the wind's drive and whirl
    Blow me along no longer,
    And the wind's a whisper at last—
Maybe I'll tell you then—
                some other time.

    When the rose's flash to the sunset
    Reels to the rack and the twist,
    And the rose is a red bygone,
    When the face I love is going
    And the gate to the end shall clang,
    And it's no use to beckon or say, "So long"—
Maybe I'll tell you then—
                some other time.

I never knew any more beautiful than you:
    I have hunted you under my thoughts,
    I have broken down under the wind
    And into the roses looking for you.
      I shall never find any
               greater than you.

Back Yard

Shine on, O moon of summer.
Shine to the leaves of grass, catalpa and oak,
All silver under your rain tonight.

An Italian boy is sending songs to you tonight from an accordion.
A Polish boy is out with his best girl; they marry next month; tonight they are
    throwing you kisses.

An old man next door is dreaming over a sheen that sits in a cherry tree in his
    back yard.

The clocks say I must go—I stay here sitting on the back porch drinking white
    thoughts you rain down.

    Shine on, O moon,
Shake out more and more silver changes.

Follies

Shaken,
The blossoms of lilac,
And shattered,
The atoms of purple.
Green dip the leaves,
Darker the bark,
Longer the shadows.

Sheer lines of poplar
Shimmer with masses of silver
And down in a garden old with years
And broken walls of ruin and story,
Roses rise with red rain-memories.
May!
In the open world
The sun comes and finds your face,
Remembering all.

Gone

Everybody loved Chick Lorimer in our town.
>Far off
>Everybody loved her.

So we all love a wild girl keeping a hold
>On a dream she wants.

Nobody knows now where Chick Lorimer went.
Nobody knows why she packed her trunk . . . a few old things
And is gone,
>Gone with her little chin
>Thrust ahead of her
>And her soft hair blowing careless
>From under a wide hat,

Dancer, singer, a laughing passionate lover.

Were there ten men or a hundred hunting Chick?
Were there five men or fifty with aching hearts?
>Everybody loved Chick Lorimer.
>Nobody knows where she's gone.

Docks

Strolling along
By the teeming docks,
I watch the ships put out.
Black ships that heave and lunge
And move like mastodons
Arising from lethargic sleep.

The fathomed harbor
Calls them not nor dares
Them to a strain of action,
But outward, on and outward,
Sounding low-reverberating calls,
Shaggy in the half-lit distance,
They pass the pointed headland,
View the wide, far-lifting wilderness
And leap with cumulative speed
To test the challenge of the sea.

Plunging,
Doggedly onward plunging,
Into salt and mist and foam and sun.

Waiting

Today I will let the old boat stand
Where the sweep of the harbor tide comes in
To the pulse of a far, deep-steady sway.
And I will rest and dream and sit on the deck
    Watching the world go by
And take my pay for many hard days gone I remember.

I will choose what clouds I like
In the great white fleets that wander the blue
As I lie on my back or loaf at the rail.
And I will listen as the veering winds kiss me and fold me
And put on my brow the touch of the world's great will.

Daybreak will hear the heart of the boat beat,
   Engine throb and piston play
In the quiver and leap at call of life.
Tomorrow we move in the gaps and heights
On changing floors of unlevel seas
And no man shall stop us and no man follow
For ours is the quest of an unknown shore
And we are husky and lusty and shouting-gay.

Dream Girl

You will come one day in a waver of love,
Tender as dew, impetuous as rain,
The tan of the sun will be on your skin,
The purr of the breeze in your murmuring speech,
You will pose with a hill-flower grace.

You will come, with your slim, expressive arms,
A poise of the head no sculptor has caught
And nuances spoken with shoulder and neck,
Your face in a pass-and-repass of moods
As many as skies in delicate change
Of cloud and blue and flimmering sun.

Yet,
You may not come, O girl of a dream,
We may but pass as the world goes by
And take from a look of eyes into eyes,
A film of hope and a memoried day.

I am the People, the Mob

I am the people—the mob—the crowd—the mass.

Do you know that all the great work of the world is done through me?

I am the workingman, the inventor, the maker of the world's food and clothes.

I am the audience that witnesses history. The Napoleons come from me and
the Lincolns. They die. And then I send forth more Napoleons and
Lincolns.

I am the seed ground. I am a prairie that will stand for much plowing. Terrible
storms pass over me. I forget. The best of me is sucked out and wasted.
I forget. Everything but Death comes to me and makes me work and give
up what I have. And I forget.

Sometimes I growl, shake myself and spatter a few red drops for history to
remember. Then—I forget.

When I, the People, learn to remember, when I, the People, use the lessons of
yesterday and no longer forget who robbed me last year, who played me
for a fool—then there will be no speaker in all the world say the name:
"The People," with any fleck of a sneer in his voice or any far-off smile
of derision.

The mob—the crowd—the mass—will arrive then.

Government

The Government—I heard about the Government and I went out to find it.
I said I would look closely at it when I saw it.

Then I saw a policeman dragging a drunken man to the calaboose. It was the Government in action.

I saw a ward alderman slip into an office one morning and talk with a judge. Later in the day the judge dismissed a case against a pickpocket who was a live ward worker for the alderman. Again I saw this was the Government, doing things.

I saw militiamen level their rifles at a crowd of workingmen who were trying to get other workingmen to stay away from a shop where there was a strike on. Government in action.

Everywhere I saw that Government is a thing made of men, that Government has blood and bones, it is many mouths whispering into many ears, sending telegrams, aiming rifles, writing orders, saying "yes" and "no."

Government dies as the men who form it die and are laid away in their graves and the new Government that comes after is human, made of heartbeats of blood, ambitions, lusts, and money running through it all, money paid and money taken, and money covered up and spoken of with hushed voices.

A Government is just as secret and mysterious and sensitive as any human sinner carrying a load of germs, traditions and corpuscles handed down from fathers and mothers away back.

The Mist

I am the mist, the impalpable mist,
Back of the thing you seek.
My arms are long,
Long as the reach of time and space.

Some toil and toil, believing,
Looking now and again on my face,
Catching a vital, olden glory.

But no one passes me,
I tangle and snare them all.
I am the cause of the Sphinx,
The voiceless, baffled, patient Sphinx.

I was at the first of things,
I will be at the last.
        I am the primal mist
        And no man passes me;
        My long impalpable arms
        Bar them all.

Early Moon

The baby moon, a canoe, a silver papoose canoe, sails and sails in the Indian west.

A ring of silver foxes, a mist of silver foxes, sit and sit around the Indian moon.

One yellow star for a runner, and rows of blue stars for more runners, keep a line of watchers.

O foxes, baby moon, runners, you are the panel of memory, fire-white writing tonight of the Red Man's dreams.

Who squats, legs crossed and arms folded, matching its look against the moon-face, the star-faces, of the West?

Who are the Mississippi Valley ghosts, of copper foreheads, riding wiry ponies in the night?—no bridles, love-arms on the pony necks, riding in the night a long old trail?

Why do they always come back when the silver foxes sit around the early moon, a silver papoose, in the Indian west?

Illinois Farmer

Bury this old Illinois farmer with respect.
He slept the Illinois nights of his life after days of work in Illinois cornfields.
Now he goes on a long sleep.
The wind he listened to in the cornsilk and the tassels, the wind that combed
his red beard zero mornings when the snow lay white on the yellow ears
in the bushel basket at the corncrib,
The same wind will now blow over the place here where his hands must
dream of Illinois corn.

Hits and Runs

I remember the Chillicothe ball players grappling the Rock Island ball players
in a sixteen-inning game ended by darkness.
And the shoulders of the Chillicothe players were a red smoke against the
sundown and the shoulders of the Rock Island players were a yellow
smoke against the sundown.
And the umpire's voice was hoarse calling balls and strikes and outs and the
umpire's throat fought in the dust for a song.

Sunset from Omaha Hotel Window

Into the blue river hills
The red sun runners go
And the long sand changes
And today is a goner
And today is not worth haggling over.

>Here in Omaha
>The gloaming is bitter
>As in Chicago
>Or Kenosha.

The long sand changes.
Today is a goner.
Time knocks in another brass nail.
Another yellow plunger shoots the dark.

>Constellations
>Wheeling over Omaha
>As in Chicago
>Or Kenosha.

The long sand is gone
      and all the talk is stars.
They circle in a dome over Nebraska.

Bilbea

(FROM TABLET WRITING, BABYLONIAN EXCAVATIONS
OF THE 4TH MILLENNIUM B.C.)

Bilbea, I was in Babylon on Saturday night.
I saw nothing of you anywhere.
I was at the old place and the other girls were there, but no Bilbea.

Have you gone to another house? or city?
Why don't you write?
I was sorry. I walked home half-sick.

Tell me how it goes.
Send me some kind of a letter.
And take care of yourself.

Portrait of a Motorcar

It's a lean car . . . a long-legged dog of a car . . . a gray-ghost eagle car.
The feet of it eat the dirt of a road . . . the wings of it eat the hills.
Danny the driver dreams of it when he sees women in red skirts and red sox
    in his sleep.
It is in Danny's life and runs in the blood of him . . . a lean gray-ghost car.

Sixteen Months

On the lips of the child Janet float changing dreams.
It is a thin spiral of blue smoke,
A morning campfire at a mountain lake.

On the lips of the child Janet,
Wisps of haze on ten miles of corn,
Young light blue calls to young light gold of morning.

Prayers of Steel

Lay me on an anvil, O God.
Beat me and hammer me into a crowbar.
Let me pry loose old walls.
Let me lift and loosen old foundations.

Lay me on an anvil, O God.
Beat me and hammer me into a steel spike.
Drive me into the girders that hold a skyscraper together.
Take red-hot rivets and fasten me into the central girders.
Let me be the great nail holding a skyscraper through blue nights into
    white stars.

Jabberers

I rise out of my depths with my language.
You rise out of your depths with your language.

Two tongues from the depths,
Alike only as a yellow cat and a greet parrot are alike,
Fling their staccato tantalizations
Into a wildcat jabber
Over a gossamer web of unanswerables.

The second and the third silence,
Even the hundredth silence,
Is better than no silence at all
(Maybe this is a jabber too—are we at it again, you and I?)

I rise out of my depths with my language.
You rise out of your depths with your language.

One thing there is much of; the name men call it by is time; into this gulf our
syllabic pronunciamentos empty by the way rockets of fire curve and are
gone on the night sky; into this gulf the jabberings go as the shower at
a scissors grinder's wheel. . . .

Knucks

In Abraham Lincoln's city,
Where they remember his lawyer's shingle,
The place where they brought him
Wrapped in battle flags,
Wrapped in the smoke of memories
From Tallahassee to the Yukon,
The place now where the shaft of his tomb
Points white against the blue prairie dome,
In Abraham Lincoln's city . . . I saw knucks
In the window of Mister Fischman's second-hand store
On Second Street.

I went in and asked, "How much?"
"Thirty cents apiece," answered Mister Fischman.
And taking a box of new ones off a shelf
He filled anew the box in the showcase
And said incidentally, most casually
And incidentally:
"I sell a carload a month of these."

I slipped my fingers into a set of knucks,
Cast-iron knucks molded in a foundry pattern,
And there came to me a set of thoughts like these:
Mister Fischman is for Abe and the "malice to none" stuff,
And the street car strikers and the strike-breakers,
And the sluggers, gunmen, detectives, policemen,
Judges, utility heads, newspapers, priests, lawyers,
They are all for Abe and the "malice to none" stuff.

I started for the door.
"Maybe you want a lighter pair,"
Came Mister Fischman's voice.
I opened the door . . . and the voice again:
"You are a funny customer."

Wrapped in battle flags,
Wrapped in the smoke of memories,
This is the place they brought him,
This is Abraham Lincoln's home town.

Testament

I give the undertakers permission to haul my body
to the graveyard and to lay away all, the head, the
feet, the hands, all: I know there is nothing left
over they can not put away.

Let the nanny goats and the billy goats of the shanty
people eat the clover over my grave and if any yellow
hair or any blue smoke of flowers is good enough to grow
over me let the dirty-fisted children of the shanty
people pick these flowers.

I have had my chance to live with the people who have
too much and the people who have too little and I chose
one of the two and I have told no man why.

Crimson Rambler

Now that a crimson rambler
     begins to crawl over the house
     of our two lives—

Now that a red curve
     winds across the shingles—

Now that hands
     washed in early sunrises
     climb and spill scarlet
     on a white lattice weave—

Now that a loop of blood
     is written on our roof
     and reaching around a chimney—

How are the two lives of this house
     to keep strong hands and strong hearts?

Haunts

There are places I go when I am strong.
One is a marsh pool where I used to go
                  with a long-ear hound-dog.
One is a wild crabapple tree; I was there
          a moonlight night with a girl.
The dog is gone; the girl is gone; I go to these
         places when there is no other place to go.

Have Me

Have me in the blue and the sun.
Have me on the open sea and the mountains.

When I go into the grass of the sea floor, I will go alone.
This is where I came from—the chlorine and the salt are blood and
    bones.
It is here the nostrils rush the air to the lungs. It is here oxygen clamors
    to be let in.
And here in the root grass of the sea floor I will go alone.

Love goes far. Here love ends.
Have me in the blue and the sun.

Fire Dreams

(WRITTEN TO BE READ ALOUD, IF SO BE, THANKSGIVING DAY)

I remember here by the fire,
In the flickering reds and saffrons,
They came in a ramshackle tub,
Pilgrims in tall hats,
Pilgrims of iron jaws,
Drifting by weeks on beaten seas,
And the random chapters say
They were glad and sang to God.
And so
Since the iron-jawed men sat down
And said, "Thanks, O God,"
For life and soup and a little less
Than a hobo handout today,
Since gray winds blew gray patterns of sleet on Plymouth Rock,
Since the iron-jawed men sang "Thanks, O God,"
You and I, O Child of the West,
Remember more than ever
November and the hunter's moon,
November and the yellow-spotted hills.

And so
In the name of the iron-jawed men
I will stand up and say yes till the finish is come and gone.
God of all broken hearts, empty hands, sleeping soldiers,
God of all star-flung beaches of night sky,
I and my love-child stand up together today and sing: "Thanks,
    O God."

Baby Face

White Moon comes in on a baby face.
The shafts across her bed are flimmering.

Out on the land White Moon shines,
Shines and glimmers against gnarled shadows,
All silver to slow twisted shadows
Falling across the long road that runs from the house.

Keep a little of your beauty
And some of your flimmering silver
For her by the window tonight
Where you come in, White Moon.

The Year

I

A storm of white petals,
Buds throwing open baby fists
Into hands of broad flowers.

II

Red roses running upward,
Clambering to the clutches of life
Soaked in crimson.

III

Rabbles of tattered leaves
Holding golden flimsy hopes
Against the tramplings
Into the pits and gullies.

IV

Hoarfrost and silence:
Only the muffling
Of winds dark and lonesome—
Great lullabies to the long sleepers.

Drumnotes

Days of the dead men, Danny.
Drum for the dead, drum on your
    remembering heart.

Jaurès, a great love-heart of France,
    a slug of lead in the red valves.
Kitchener of Khartoum, tall, cold, proud,
    a shark's mouthful.
Franz Josef, the old man of forty haunted
    kingdoms, in a tomb with the Hapsburg
    fathers, moths eating a green uniform
    to tatters, worms taking all and leaving
    only bones and gold buttons, bones and
    iron crosses.
Jack London, Jim Riley, Verhaeren, riders to
    the republic of dreams.

Days of the dead, Danny.
Drum on your remembering heart.

Cool Tombs

When Abraham Lincoln was shoveled into the tombs, he forgot the copper-
heads and the assassin . . . in the dust, in the cool tombs.

And Ulysses Grant lost all thought of con men and Wall Street, cash and
collateral turned ashes . . . in the dust, in the cool tombs.

Pocahontas' body, lovely as a poplar, sweet as a red haw in November or a
pawpaw in May, did she wonder? does she remember? . . . in the dust, in
the cool tombs?

Take any streetful of people buying clothes and groceries, cheering a hero or
throwing confetti and blowing tin horns . . . tell me if the lovers are losers
. . . tell me if any get more than the lovers . . . in the dust . . . in the cool
tombs.

Shenandoah

In the Shenandoah Valley, one rider gray and one rider blue, and the sun on the riders wondering.

Piled in the Shenandoah, riders blue and riders gray, piled with shovels, one and another, dust in the Shenandoah taking them quicker than mothers take children done with play.

The blue nobody remembers, the gray nobody remembers, it's all old and old nowadays in the Shenandoah.

. . .

And all is young, a butter of dandelions slung on the turf, climbing blue flowers of the wishing woodlands wondering: a midnight purple violet claims the sun among old heads, among old dreams of repeating heads of a rider blue and a rider gray in the Shenandoah.

New Feet

Empty battlefields keep their phantoms.
Grass crawls over old gun wheels
And a nodding Canada thistle flings a purple
Into the summer's southwest wind,
Wrapping a root in the rust of a bayonet,
Reaching a blossom in rust of shrapnel.

Old Osawatomie

John Brown's body under the morning stars.
Six feet of dust under the morning stars.
And a panorama of war performs itself
Over the six-foot stage of circling armies.
Room for Gettysburg, Wilderness, Chickamauga,
On a six-foot stage of dust.

Grass

Pile the bodies high at Austerlitz and Waterloo.
Shovel them under and let me work—
>   I am the grass; I cover all.

And pile them high at Gettysburg
And pile them high at Ypres and Verdun.
Shovel them under and let me work.
Two years, ten years, and passengers ask the conductor:
>   What place is this?
>   Where are we now?

>   I am the grass.
>   Let me work.

Flanders

Flanders, the name of a place, a country of people,
Spells itself with letters, is written in books.

"Where is Flanders?" was asked one time,
Flanders known only to those who lived there
And milked cows and made cheese and spoke the home language.

"Where is Flanders? was asked.
And the slang adepts shot the reply: Search me.

A few thousand people milking cows, raising radishes,
On a land of salt grass and dunes, sand-swept with a sea-breath on it:
This was Flanders, the unknown, the quiet,
The place where cows hunted lush cuds of green on lowlands,
And the raw-boned plowmen took horses with long shanks
Out in the dawn to the sea-breath.

Flanders sat slow-spoken amid slow-swung windmills,
Slow-circling windmill arms turning north or west,
Turning to talk to the swaggering winds, the childish winds,
So Flanders sat with the heart of a kitchen girl
Washing wooden bowls in the winter sun by a window.

Old Timers

I am an ancient reluctant conscript.

On the soup wagons of Xerxes I was a cleaner of pans.

On the march of Miltiades' phalanx I had a haft and head;
I had a bristling gleaming spear-handle.

Red-headed Cæsar picked me for a teamster.
He said, "Go to work, you Tuscan bastard,
Rome calls for a man who can drive horses."

The units of conquest led by Charles the Twelfth,
The whirling whimsical Napoleonic columns:
They saw me one of the horseshoers.

I trimmed the feet of a white horse Bonaparte swept the night stars with.

Lincoln said, "Get into the game; your nation takes you."
And I drove a wagon and team and I had my arm shot off
At Spotsylvania Court House.

I am an ancient reluctant conscript.

Remembered Women

For a woman's face remembered as a spot of quick light on the flat land of dark night,

For this memory of one mouth and a forehead they go on in the gray rain and the mud, they go on among the boots and guns.

The horizon ahead is a thousand fang flashes, it is a row of teeth that bite on the flanks of night, the horizon sings of a new kill and a big kill.

The horizon behind is a wall of dark etched with a memory, fixed with a woman's face—they fight on and on, boots in the mud and heads in the gray rain—for the women they hate and the women they love—for the women they left behind, they fight on.

A Million Young Workmen, 1915

A million young workmen straight and strong lay stiff on the grass and roads,
And the million are now under soil and their rotting flesh will in the years feed
    roots of blood-red roses.
Yes, this million of young workmen slaughtered one another and never saw
    their red hands.
And oh, it would have been a great job of killing and a new and beautiful thing
    under the sun if the million knew why they hacked and tore each other
    to death.
The kings are grinning, the kaiser and the czar—they are alive riding in
    leather-seated motor cars, and they have their women and roses for ease,
    and they eat fresh poached eggs for breakfast, new butter on toast, sitting
    in tall water-tight houses reading the news of war.
I dreamed a million ghosts of the young workmen rose in their shirts all soaked
    in crimson . . . and yelled:
God damn the grinning kings, God damn the kaiser and the czar.

[CHICAGO, 1915]

82

The Four Brothers

NOTES FOR WAR SONGS (NOVEMBER, 1917)

Make war songs out of these;
Make chants that repeat and weave.
Make rhythms up to the ragtime chatter of the machine guns;
Make slow-booming psalms up to the boom of the big guns.
Make a marching song of swinging arms and swinging legs,
      Going along,
      Going along,
On the roads from San Antonio to Athens, from Seattle to Bagdad—
The boys and men in winding lines of khaki, the circling squares of
    bayonet points.

Cowpunchers, cornhuskers, shopmen, ready in khaki;
Ballplayers, lumberjacks, ironworkers, ready in khaki;
A million, ten million, singing, "I am ready."
This the sun looks on between two seaboards,
In the land of Lincoln, in the land of Grant and Lee.

I heard one say, "I am ready to be killed."
I heard another say, "I am ready to be killed."
O sunburned clear-eyed boys!
I stand on sidewalks and you go by with drums and guns and bugles,
      You—and the flag!

And my heart tightens, a fist of something feels my throat
      When you go by,
You on the kaiser hunt, you and your faces saying, "I am ready to be killed."

They are hunting death,
Death for the one-armed mastoid kaiser.
They are after a Hohenzollern head:
There is no man-hunt of men remembered like this.
The four big brothers are out to kill.
France, Russia, Britain, America—
The four republics are sworn brothers to kill the kaiser.

Yes, this is the great man-hunt;
And the sun has never seen till now
Such a line of toothed and tusked man-killers,
In the blue of the upper sky,
In the green of the undersea,
In the red of winter dawns.
Eating to kill,
Sleeping to kill,
Asked by their mothers to kill,
Wished by four-fifths of the world to kill—
To cut the kaiser's throat,
To hack the kaiser's head,
To hang the kaiser on a high-horizon gibbet.

And is it nothing else than this?
Three times ten million men thirsting the blood
Of a half-cracked one-armed child of the German kings?
Three times ten million men asking the blood
Of a child born with his head wrong-shaped,
The blood of rotted kings in his veins?
If this were all, O God,
I would go to the far timbers

And look on the gray wolves
Tearing the throats of moose:
I would ask a wilder drunk of blood.

Look! It is four brothers in joined hands together.
> The people of bleeding France,
> The people of bleeding Russia,
> The people of Britain, the people of America—
These are the four brothers, these are the four republics.

At first I said it in anger as one who clenches his fist in wrath to fling his
    knuckles into the face of some one taunting;
Now I say it calmly as one who has thought it over and over again at night,
    among the mountains, by the sea-combers in storm.
I say now, by God, only fighters today will save the world, nothing but fighters
    will keep alive the names of those who left red prints of bleeding feet at
    Valley Forge in Christmas snow.
On the cross of Jesus, the sword of Napoleon, the skull of Shakespeare, the
    pen of Tom Jefferson, the ashes of Abraham Lincoln, or any sign of the
    red and running life poured out by the mothers of the world,
By the God of morning glories climbing blue the doors of quiet homes, by the
    God of tall hollyhocks laughing glad to children in peaceful valleys, by the
    God of new mothers wishing peace to sit at windows nursing babies,
I swear only reckless men, ready to throw away their lives by hunger,
    deprivation, desperate clinging to a single purpose imperturbable and
    undaunted, men with the primitive guts of rebellion,
Only fighters gaunt with the red brand of labor's sorrow on their brows and
    labor's terrible pride in their blood, men with souls asking danger—only
    these will save and keep the four big brothers.

Good-night is the word, good-night to the kings, to the czars,
> Good-night to the kaiser.
The breakdown and the fade-away begins.
The shadow of a great broom, ready to sweep out the trash, is here.

One finger is raised that counts the czar,
The ghost who beckoned men who come no more—
The czar gone to the winds on God's great dustpan,
The czar a pinch of nothing,
The last of the gibbering Romanoffs.

Out and good-night—
The ghosts of the summer palaces
And the ghosts of the winter palaces!
Out and out, good-night to the kings, the czars, the kaisers.

Another finger will speak,
And the kaiser, the ghost who gestures a hundred million sleeping-
        waking ghosts,
The kaiser will go onto God's great dustpan—
The last of the gibbering Hohenzollerns.
Look! God pities this trash, God waits with a broom and a dustpan,
God knows a finger will speak and count them out.

It is written in the stars;
It is spoken on the walls;
It clicks in the fire-white zigzag of the Atlantic wireless;
It mutters in the bastions of thousand-mile continents;
It sings in a whistle on the midnight winds from Walla Walla to Mesopotamia:
Out and good-night.

The millions slow in khaki,
The millions learning *Turkey in the Straw* and *John Brown's Body*,
The millions remembering windrows of dead at Gettysburg, Chickamauga,
        and Spotsylvania Court House,
The millions dreaming of the morning star of Appomattox,
The millions easy and calm with guns and steel, planes and prows:
        There is a hammering, drumming hell to come.
        The killing gangs are on the way.

God takes one year for a job.
God takes ten years or a million.
God knows when a doom is written.
God knows this job will be done and the words spoken:
Out and good-night.
> The red tubes will run,
> And the great price be paid,
> And the homes empty,
> And the wives wishing,
> And the mothers wishing.
There is only one way now, only the way of the red tubes and the
    great price.

> Well . . .
Maybe the morning sun is a five-cent yellow balloon,
And the evening stars the joke of a God gone crazy.
Maybe the mothers of the world,
And the life that pours from their torsal folds—
Maybe it's all a lie sworn by liars,
And a God with a cackling laughter says:
"I, the Almighty God,
I have made all this,
I have made it for kaisers, czars, and kings."

Three times ten million men say: No.
Three times ten million men say:
> God is a God of the People.
And the God who made the world
> And fixed the morning sun,
> And flung the evening stars,
> And shaped the baby hands of life,
This is the God of the Four Brothers;
This is the God of bleeding France and bleeding Russia;
This is the God of the people of Britain and America.

The graves from the Irish Sea to the Caucasus peaks are ten times a million.

The stubs and stumps of arms and legs, the eyesockets empty, the cripples, ten times a million.

The crimson thumb-print of this anathema is on the door panels of a hundred million homes.

Cows gone, mothers on sick-beds, children cry a hunger and no milk comes in the noon-time or at night.

The death-yells of it all, the torn throats of men in ditches calling for water, the shadows and the hacking lungs in dugouts, the steel paws that clutch and squeeze a scarlet drain day by day—the storm of it is hell.

But look! child! the storm is blowing for a clean air.

Look! the four brothers march
And hurl their big shoulders
And swear the job shall be done.

Out of the wild finger-writhing north and south, east and west, over the blood-crossed, blood-dusty ball of earth,

Out of it all a God who knows is sweeping clean,

Out of it all a God who sees and pierces through, is breaking and cleaning out an old thousand years, is making ready for a new thousand years.

The four brothers shall be five and more.

Under the chimneys of the winter-time the children of the world shall sing new songs.

Among the rocking restless cradles the mothers of the world shall sing new sleepy-time songs.

Index of First Lines

A million young workmen straight and strong lay stiff on the grass and roads	82
Among the mountains I wandered and saw blue haze and red crag and was amazed	4
A stone face higher than six horses stood five thousand years gazing at the world seeming to clutch a secret.	22
A storm of white petals	73
Bilbea, I was in Babylon on Saturday night.	62
Bury this old Illinois farmer with respect.	60
By day the skyscraper looms in the smoke and sun and has a soul.	33
Come you, cartoonists	7
Cross the hands over the breast here—so.	18
Days of the dead men, Danny	74
Desolate and lone	5
Dust of the feet	8
Empty battlefields keep their phantoms.	77
Everybody loved Chick Lorimer in our town.	52
Flanders, the name of a place, a country of people	79
For a woman's face remembered as a spot of quick light on the flat land of dark night	81
For the gladness here where the sun is shining at evening on the weeds at the river	46
Give me hunger	47
Good-by now to the streets and the clash of wheels and locking hubs	10
Guns	38
Have me in the blue and the sun.	70
High noon. White sun flashes on the Michigan Avenue asphalt.	29
Hog Butcher for the World	1

89

I am an ancient reluctant conscript. 80

I am riding on a limited express, one of the crack trains of the nation. 22

I am the mist, the impalpable mist 58

I am the people—the mob—the crowd—the mass. 56

I asked professors who teach the meaning of life to tell me what is happiness. 11

I cannot tell you now 49

I drank musty ale at the Illinois Athletic Club with the millionaire manufacturer of Green River butter one night 25

I dreamed one man stood against a thousand 43

I give the undertakers permission to haul my body 68

I have been watching the war map slammed up for advertising in front of the newspaper office. 40

I know a Jew fish crier down on Maxwell Street with a voice like a north wind blowing over corn stubble in January. 10

I know an ice handler who wears a flannel shirt with pearl buttons the size of a dollar 24

In Abraham Lincoln's city 66

In the old wars drum of hoofs and the beat of shod feet. 41

In the Shenandoah Valley, one rider gray and one rider blue, and the sun on the riders wondering. 76

Into the blue river hills 61

I remember here by the fire 71

I remember the Chillicothe ball players grappling the Rock Island ball players in a sixteen-inning game ended by darkness. 60

I rise out of my depths with my language. 65

I sat with a dynamiter at supper in a German saloon eating steak and onions. 23

I shall foot it 42

It's a lean car . . . a long-legged dog of a car . . . a gray-ghost eagle car. 63

I wanted a man's face looking into the jaws and throat of life 44

John Brown's body under the morning stars. 77

Lay me on an anvil, O God. 64

Little one, you have been buzzing in the books 32

Make war songs out of these 83

Mamie beat her head against the bars of a little Indiana town and dreamed of
    romance and big things off somewhere the way the railroad trains all ran.   19

Mrs. Gabrielle Giovannitti comes along Peoria Street every morning at nine
    o'clock   15

My head knocks against the stars.   45

New-mown hay smell and wind of the plain made her a woman whose ribs had
    the power of the hills in them   17

Now that a crimson rambler   69

Of my city the worse that men will ever say is this   6

Once when I saw a cripple   18

On the lips of the child Janet float changing dreams.   63

Out of the fire   36

Passers-by   9

Passing through huddled and ugly walls   5

Pile the bodies high at Austerlitz and Waterloo.   78

Red drips from my chin where I have been eating   39

Riding against the east   28

Sand of the sea runs red   37

Shaken   51

Shine on, O moon of summer.   50

Storms have beaten on this point of land   20

Strolling along   53

Style—go ahead talking about style.   27

Sunday night and the park policemen tell each other it is dark as a stack of
    black cats on Lake Michigan.   11

Take your fill of intimate remorse, perfumed sorrow   13

The baby moon, a canoe, a silver papoose canoe, sails and sails in the Indian
    west.   59

The bronze General Grant riding a bronze horse in Lincoln Park   30

The fog comes   36

The Government—I heard about the Government and I went out to find it.   59

There are places I go when I am strong.   70

There's Chamfort. He's a sample.   21

The shadows of the ships   3

The single clenched fist lifted and ready   36

Today I will let the old boat stand   54

Tomb of a millionaire   12

Under the harvest moon   48

What do we see here in the sand dunes of the white moon alone with our
    thoughts, Bill   31

When Abraham Lincoln was shoveled into the tombs, he forgot the
    copperheads and the assassin   75

White Moon comes in on a baby face.   72

Yellow dust on a bumble bee's wing   37

Your whitelight flashes the frost tonight   37

You will come out one day in a waver of love   55